Choose Love

I welcome you

to a series of contemplative meditations.
There are 31 daily reflections for you
to experience fresh encounters
with Love throughout the month.
These photos were taken
while I was on an awakening journey with Love.
As you linger with Love throughout these pages,
may what happened for me also be for you.
A passage of grace opened
into the depths of refreshing springs of Living Water.
Let yourself be led far beyond a sip or a cup;
where you actually become a bubbling well!
As you gaze, ponder, and pray, may you be present and open to
new wonders with the mysterious presence of God.
Love will illuminate your beautiful diamond soul.

Love upon Love,
Lorie

You are invited to .....

Enter,

Engage,

Experience

Encounter

and Embrace

Love

Each daily meditation holds the following components that are designed to deepen your contemplative experience.
Begin with a quiet place and settle into the silence, noticing your body and breath. As you enter into a prayerful experience with the photo and writing, you will discover Divine Love through images and symbols; through stillness and beauty.

Photo ~ As you look at the photo, notice the image of the heart shape found in nature allowing your gaze to deepen.
Become aware of what feelings are emerging for you as you linger in the Presence of Love.

Quote / Poem ~ As you read the writing for the day, allow the message to unfold in your imagination and notice if it evokes any memories, feelings, or other images.
Become aware of what part(s) of the words and photo touch in you.

Pause & Ponder ~ Be still with what calls or challenges you.
Create spaciousness within you to hold what is stirring.
As you ponder, let yourself be drawn into deeper reflection.
Notice your desire to grow in intimacy with yourself and The Beloved. Take a few moments to let this sink in.

Prayer ~ How do you want to respond to the images, words, thoughts, memories, and invitations from Love?
As you are held in Love, slowly and intentionally say the sentence prayer that is given, or create your own, as a loving response to God.
You may want to take this prayer with you into the day.

Breathe in ~ Nurture your relationship with God by deeply breathing in these next words, or stay with the prayer if it is more meaningful to your experience.
After you have connected with the invitation that is being extended to you, responded in prayer, and breathed deeply of Love, begin to release all the words and images.
Close your eyes for a few moments, breathe restfully, savor the quiet darkness as you continue surrendering to Love.
Rest in a peaceful awareness of God's loving presence.
Allow your breathing to bring you to a time to **simply be**.

Personal Word for Today ~ What word, phrase, or image are you taking with you from this lingering with Love?
Write it on the line provided and in your journal for further reflection. You may want to write it on a sticky note and take it with you for the day. You can find an object that symbolizes what you have been given and put it in a prominent place.
Let Love continue to ruminate by the Spirit within you.
Name what is happening and cherish it.

If thoughts or artistic expressions emerge (a sketch, poem, or song ...) from the day's meditation be sure to capture them in your journal or create a piece that will deepen the grace given.

"God wants nothing more than our consent to be loved."

Thomas Keating

"Love bade me welcome ..."

George Herbert

Pause & Ponder ~ God constantly initiates

love toward me.

Prayer ~ I say " Yes" to Love in these new beginnings.

Breathe in ~ I am wanted - as I am.

Personal Word for Today ~ _____

"Behold The Beholder

Beholding you ..... and smiling"

Anthony deMello

Pause & Ponder ~ Being gazed upon by Love.
Prayer ~ Let this truth soak into my bones.
Breathe in ~ I am Seen. Accepted. Cherished.

My Word for Today ~_____

"How gently and lovingly
you wake in my heart,
where in secret you dwell alone;
and in your sweet breathing,
filled with good and glory,
how tenderly you swell my heart with Love."

St. John of the Cross

Pause & Ponder ~ The gentle swell of Love within me.
Prayer ~ Awaken me to the great beauty of Love.
Breathe in ~ "I Love You," from the Beloved
in each breath; and offer it back as you breathe out.

Personal Word for Today ~ _____

"Generous God,
I come to you again, holding out my waiting cup,
begging that it first be emptied
of all that blocks the way, then asking for its filling with
love that tastes like you."

Joyce Rupp

Pause & Ponder ~ I am a waiting cup to God.
Prayer ~ My longing is that I may taste your love.
Breathe in ~ The filling of Love to my very depths.

Personal Word for Today ~ _____

"God is nearer to us than our own soul,
for he is the ground on which our soul stands ...
for our soul sits in God in complete rest
and our soul stands in God in complete strength
and our soul is naturally rooted in God in eternal love."

Julian of Norwich

Pause & Ponder ~ God is intimately near.
Prayer ~ May I experience complete rest and strength.
Breathe in ~ I am rooted in Eternal Love.

Personal Word for Today ~ _____

"Grace always comes .....
She is a Fierce Lover."

Lorie Martin

Pause & Ponder ~ What is the grace I seek today?
Prayer ~ I open to receive what is offered to me.
Breathe in ~ Grace upon grace; full of light and hope.

Personal Word for today ~ _____

"Remain in my Love"

Jesus

Pause & Ponder ~ Remain: to stay in the same place or
    with the same person or group; after others have gone.
Prayer ~ May I be still and linger with You.
Breathe ~ I am at home in Love .

Personal Word for Today ~ _____

"...suddenly everywhere present,
overflowed the heart,
and washed my eyes
that were almost blind under the dust."

Simone Weil

Pause & Ponder ~ What is the dust on my eyes?
Prayer ~ Fill my heart that I may see newness of life.
Breathe in ~ The endless spring of Love.

Personal Word for Today ~ _____

" 'You must sit down', says Love, 'and taste my meat.'
So I did sit and eat."

George Herbert

Pause & Ponder ~ What do I notice when I sit down?
Prayer ~ Let me rest with you and taste your goodness.
Breathe in ~ I surrender as Love serves me.

Personal Word for Today ~ _____

"I tasted everything.
I found nothing better than you.
When I dove into the sea,
I found no pearl like you.
I opened casks,
I tasted jars,
Yet none but that rebellious wine of yours
touched my lips and inspired my heart."

Rumi

Pause & Ponder ~ Diving into the sea.
Prayer ~ Inspire my heart that my inner world be aglow.
Breathe in ~ The sacred wine of Divine Love.

Personal Word for Today ~ _____

"We are love, and we are made for love,
and our natural abiding place is love."

Richard Rohr

Pause & Ponder ~ I am made for love.
Prayer ~ I make my home in Love.
Breathe in ~ I am love; I love.

Personal Word for Today ~ _____

"I will wait ..... for you."

Mumford & Sons

Pause & Ponder ~ What am I waiting for?
Prayer ~ Hold me close all the while I wait.
Breathe in ~ It will be worth the wait.

Personal Word for Today ~ _____

"In the place of purified love,
all things are drawn together
and choose to move harmoniously
in a dance, energized by love."

Jeff Imbach

Pause & Ponder ~ A harmonious dance.
Prayer ~ Recover me with energized love.
Breathe in ~ You draw me close and I dance.

Personal Word for Today ~ _____

"To live in this world
you must be able to do three things:
to love what is mortal;
to hold it against your bones
knowing your own life depends on it;
and, when the time comes to let it go,
to let it go."

Mary Oliver

Pause & Ponder ~ What do I hold against my bones?
Prayer ~ I ask for the grace to let go what I must.
Breathe In ~ The ardent love of letting go.

Personal Word for Today ~ _____

"God has two arms with which He holds and embraces.
One is His omnipotent protection,
by which He supports.
The other is the perfect love with which He embraces ...
... this divine embrace will continue throughout eternity."

Jeanne Guyon

Pause & Ponder ~ The *arms* of God around me.
Prayer ~ Support me inside and encircle me all around.
Breathe in ~ I am held and embraced.

Personal Word for Today ~ _____

"Limitless love,
from the depths to the stars: flooding all, loving all.
It is the royal kiss of peace."

Hildegard of Bingen

Pause & Ponder ~ Limitless love.
Prayer ~ I receive your kiss of peace.
Breathe in ~ Love from the deep to the stars.

Personal Word for Today _____

"Many waters cannot quench love;
Rivers cannot wash it away."

Song of Songs

Pause & Ponder ~ I am being given unquenchable love.
Prayer ~ May I live this kind of love as my reality.
Breathe in ~ Unmoveable Love.

Personal Word for Today ~ _____

"Holy Light, Sacred Fire, Glorious Breath,

My soul awakens as a flower surrenders to the sun."

Lorie Martin

Pause & Ponder ~ Surrendering to the sun.
Prayer ~ Awaken me.
Breathe in ~ The warm breath of Sacred Fire.

Personal Word for Today ~ _____

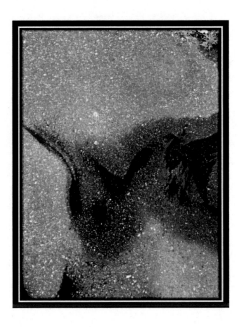

"Place your mind before the mirror of eternity!
Place your soul in the brilliance of glory!
Place your heart in the image of the divine substance...
And taste the hidden sweetness that God has reserved
for his lovers."

Clare of Assisi

Pause & Ponder ~ The mirror of eternity.
Prayer ~ I place my soul in the brilliance of glory.
Breathe in ~ Loves hidden sweetness.

Personal Word for Today ~ _____

"It is our ordinary work to care for
our extra-ordinary souls."

Lorie Martin

Pause & Ponder ~ The beauty of my own soul.
Prayer ~ Guide me as I care for the glory of who I am.
Breathe in ~ I offer devoted care to my precious soul.

Personal Word for Today ~ _____

"But you, MacKenzie, you were made to be loved."

Papa, "The Shack" ~ Wm. Paul Young

Pause & Ponder ~ Do I believe I am loved?
Prayer ~ Come to the "knot-hole" of pain
                                    that I live through.
Breathe in ~ The pure healing light of Love.

Personal Word for Today ~ _____

"Love is the strongest force the world possesses
Yet it is the humblest imaginable."

Mahatma Gandhi

Pause & Ponder ~ The strong energy force of Love.
Prayer ~ Guide me to love humbly and strong.
Breathe in ~ The strength of Beautiful Love

Personal Word for Today ~ _____

"My eyes are closed;
yet I'm wide awake
in love, in awe."

Lorie Martin

Pause & Ponder ~ Being awake with your eyes closed.
Prayer ~ Awaken me even more to your gentle love.
Breathe in ~ New dawning Light.

Personal Word for today ~ _____

"I open my heart to Love"

Cathy A. J. Hardy

Pause & Ponder ~ Wandering in the woods.
Prayer ~ Free me that I may be free to love.
Breathe in ~ I align my heart with Love.

Personal Word for Today ~ _____

"O I love Him!
My God, I Love You."

Final words of St. Therese of Lisieux

Pause & Ponder ~ The reality of my love for God.
Prayer ~ I love you.
Breathe in ~ The true interactive Love of God.

Personal Word for Today ~_____

"Don't let yourself lose me.
Nearby is the country they call Life.
You will know it ... Give me your hand."

Ranier Maria Rilke

Pause & Ponder ~ Being led by the hand.
Prayer ~ Let me follow you into new lands of Life.
Breathe in ~ The dance of Life.

Personal Word for Today ~ _____

"Be not afraid, My love is stronger
My love is stronger than your fear
Be not afraid, My love is stronger
And I have promised
Promised to be always near"

Song by John Bell, Iona Community

Pause & Ponder ~ How might I fear Love?
Prayer ~ Help me see Truth and be at peace.
Breathe in ~ The nearness of God.

Personal Word for Today ~ _____

"I want to pour out my love extravagantly on you.
Look at the waves lapping upon the shore.
My love is even more consistent
than their constant rhythm.
Let my love wash over you like waves." ~ Jesus

Eden Jersak

Pause & Ponder ~ The waves lapping upon the shore.
Prayer ~ I consent to your ever-flowing love.
Breathe in ~ Extravagant Love without measure.

Personal Word for Today ~ _____

"Because of the Beloved
my heart is happy, my soul illuminated.
From the beloved's greenery
hundreds of blessed rivers
are flowing to the rose gardens.
In order to enter into your rose garden,
the soul makes peace with the thorns.
Choose love. Choose love.
Without this beautiful love,
life is nothing but a burden."

~ Rumi

Pause & Ponder ~ Making peace with the thorns.
Prayer ~ I choose love.
Breathe in ~ Light & healing love to my rose garden.

Personal Word for Today ~ _____

"Fall in love, stay in love,
and it will decide everything."

Father Pedro Arrupe

Pause & Ponder ~ Fresh Life with sturdy roots.
Prayer ~ Grace me with a deepened trust.
Breathe in ~ I am in Love.

Personal Word for Today ~ _____

"My lover spoke and said to me,
"Arise, my darling, my beautiful one, and come with me.
See! The winter is past; the rains are over and gone.
Flowers appear on the earth;
the season of singing has come,
the cooing of doves is heard in our land."

Song of Songs

Pause & Ponder ~ The season of singing.
Prayer ~ I have come.
Breathe in ~ The presence and voice of my Beloved.

Personal Word for Today ~ _____

Created with
Deepest Gratitude
for
The Grand Embrace of Divine Love

Lorie Martin

November 2015

www.loriemartin.com

invitedin@telus.net

Made in the USA
San Bernardino, CA
24 January 2016